# West Yorkshire C

## *on old picture postcards*

### Norman Ellis

**1.** An interested crowd witnesses the transportation by traction engine of a 20 feet diameter headgear pulley, weighing 10 tons, as it passes the "George & Dragon," Hemsworth, en route for **Frickley Colliery,** South Elmsall, on 30th April 1906. The makers were Qualters & Smith Brothers, Old Foundry, Barnsley.

£3.95

<< Skipton

Goole >>

●Bradford

●Garforth

●Wyke

●Morley

●Ledston Luck
●Rothwell

●Robin Hood

●Castleford

Ardsley●

●Whitwood

Batley●

Lofthouse●

●Stanley
●Altofts

●Featherstone Main
●Ackton Hall

Liversedge●

●Dewsbury

●Wakefield

Ainley Main

Shaw Cross●

●Old Roundwood

●Nostell

●Fitzwilliam
●Kinsley
●Hemsworth

●Upton

●Thornhill

●Crigglestone

●Huddersfield

●Woolley (Darton Main)
●Clayton West

●South Kirkby

●Emley Moor
●Skelmanthorpe

●South Elmsall (Frickley)

*Not to scale*

**LOCATIONS** *featured in this book*

The Main Colliery. Featherstone.

**2.** Men and lads leave **Featherstone Main Colliery** after a day shift, c. 1910. The workforce at this colliery totalled 2,500 in the early 1920s. The village, which had two collieries, boasted its own shops, including Maypole and Meadow, railway station, theatre (which became a cinema), swimming baths and the famous Featherstone Rovers rugby league team.

# Introduction

In the 1930s, as I laid in my cosy bed before the streets were aired (as my granny said), I used to listen to the colliers as they trudged to the local pit. The sound of their clogs or heavy boots was distinct and eerie. I rolled over, knowing that I need not leave my warm bed for another three hours to go to school. Sometimes, in the afternoon, I saw the same men coming home, their faces black with coal dust. I lived in Outwood, just north of Wakefield. The colliery was Lofthouse, known locally as Loftus. I would not have described Outwood, Lofthouse or Lofthouse Gate as typical pit villages, although many of their menfolk worked at Lofthouse Colliery. Certainly, the colliery was instrumental in the area's development.

My maternal grandfather, a collier, had moved from the Barnsley area to Outwood. His father had also been a coal miner. Grandad tried to build up a newspaper round in Outwood, but gave it up because of the hassle. He became a pillar of local society, was a staunch Wesleyan, but for his bread-and-butter and bringing up his six children, remained a collier. I never saw him because he died in 1927, aged 68. His pit lamp and coal pick languished in our garden shed for another three decades. I still have most of his collection of postcards, including the view of Lofthouse Colliery *(illustration 6)*. Grandfather's only son, Albert, worked at Lofthouse Colliery, eventually rising to the position of deputy. He was known to his workmates as Chipper. His five sisters, including my mother, worked at mills in the Ardsley and Morley area.

After her marriage, my mother, in common with other housewives on our council estate, hung out the washing every Monday in the garden to dry. The whiter-than-white sheets and pillowslips frequently got speckled with soot smuts. She blamed the chimney at the colliery. It was more likely that the spots came from the house chimneys, because everyone was burning coal. The coal was delivered in high-sided horse-drawn carts and tipped into the recipient's yard or on the pavement. It had to be shovelled into the coalhouse or cellar. Later, bagged coal made life a bit easier.

I progressed from Outwood Council School to Rothwell Grammar School, which was situated in another colliery area. The school, then only a few years old, had suffered because some of its teachers had been called up for war service. This resulted in the headmaster, Mr E.R. Manley, occasionally having to take a class. I think Gaffer (as we knew him) enjoyed this. He failed miserably, though, in trying to instil in me an appreciation of the works of William Shakespeare, and particularly A *Midsummer Night's Dream*. Perhaps I was the failure. I did not know at the time (1945 and 1946) that Mr Manley was researching local collieries and the men who worked in them. The result was a book entitled **Meet the Miner** which he published himself in 1947. I recently managed to buy a second-hand copy. It is a fascinating read. In his foreword, Mr Manley wrote:

*"It is over 25 years since I first met the sons of miners in my classes, but it was not till the recent war that I made close contact of an informal kind with the men themselves. During nights on duty with ARP and Home Guard, ideas which have been in my mind for a long time began to crystallise and I decided that, when the war was over, I should put them on paper. The first time I went down a Yorkshire mine, a deputy to whom I was introduced at the entry to his district said very cordially, 'I've heard of thee. Welcome to t'pit.' He was killed three weeks later in one of those casual accidents which make so little stir. To him and to his fellows in the pits of Yorkshire, I should like to dedicate this book."*

Towards the end of my days at Rothwell Grammar School, I was included in a party of boys who toured the nearby Robin Hood Coke Works *(illustration 57)*. These were connected to Robin Hood Colliery *(illustration on back cover)* by a railway across the main road. After we had negotiated several elevated walkways, we arrived at the ammonia plant. The guide lifted a lid from a drum of ammonia and asked us, one by one, to sniff it. My turn came. It was so strong that I nearly fell back over a parapet. It certainly cleared my head.

*(continued)*

**3. Darton Main Colliery** at Woolley. The card, published by Warner Gothard of Barnsley, was produced to celebrate the reaching of the Parkgate seam on 11th August 1914, according to the inscription on the kibble. The pit sinkers are shown wearing distinctive oilskins. The colliery closed in 1987.

**4.** Several small pits in the Elland area, including **Ainley Main Colliery,** provided coal for mill and home use. Here, during the 1912 dispute, when one million miners were on strike nationwide, a policeman keeps watch as men salvage poor-quality fuel from a small spoil heap.

## Introduction *(continued)*

Apart from producing coal and its by-products, the village of Robin Hood also supported extensive brick workings.

I remember Gaffer asking me in my final term what I wanted to become. I had no idea, but I was good at art. So, having obtained my School Certificate, I drifted into my first job, an apprentice draughtsman at a now long-defunct company called Hepburn Conveyor in Wakefield. The firm had been much involved in making conveyors and elevators for collieries, and possessed a lot of beautiful old drawings of them, some on linen, others in colour. The oldest drawings had been rolled into bundles and relegated to a huge dusty storeroom, two walls of which were provided with 'pigeonholes' to take them. The rolls were indexed in case anything was needed again. One day, a fairly recent drawing went missing. It was thought it may have been rolled up accidentally with older drawings and 'pigeonholed'. I wasn't blamed but was held responsible. I and another lad spent four whole days in the dusty storeroom trying to find it. In so doing, I became familiar with the 'works of art,' some of them depicting old Welsh collieries. We never found the misplaced drawing.

After three years, I moved to Woodhead Monroe (later Woodhead Manufacturing) in Ossett, a firm which made shock absorbers. No colliery connection there. But the bus I caught from Wakefield to Ossett went past Bradley & Craven, at whose now-defunct factory on the edge of Wakefield my father worked. They used to make headgear pulleys, winding engines and cages for collieries. The bus also passed Old Roundwood Colliery *(illustration 17)* and was frequently held up by a steam engine and its coal wagons as they crossed the road and headed for the main line at Low Laithes.

One George William Collier worked at Woodheads. Before the closure of nearby Shaw Cross Colliery *(illustration 16)* he worked in the weigh office there. One morning, a weights and measures inspector arrived from Bradford to check the weighbridge. George, wishing to be polite, offered him a cheery, *"Good morning."* Whereupon the inspector replied, *"If you think you can get round me like that, you're mistaken."* George remonstrated, *"If that's your attitude, I don't care whether you pass the thing or not. I'll still get paid for the time I can't use it."* The inspector failed the apparatus; it was out of use for a period, but George still got paid.

In geological terms, the West Yorkshire coalfield is part of the large Yorkshire and Midlands coalfield. The general progression was eastwards towards the deeper seams. Old Ordnance Survey maps show numerous long-vanished coal pits, many of which were small bell pits or drift mines. Their details are scanty or non-existent. By the beginning of the twentieth century, large coal mines had become established throughout West Yorkshire. A century later, deep mining in the area has virtually ceased and a way of life has ended. A large colliery wheel has been erected beside the main Leeds Road through Outwood, in memory of the men who perished in the 1973 disaster at Lofthouse Colliery. It perpetuates the memory of a larger struggle between colliers, coal owners and the cataclysmic forces of nature.

Colliery and colliery-related postcards, particularly photographic ones, have become a prized source for research and illustration. For a fraction of the current value of any one colliery postcard, this book presents a selection of over 60, collected by me over a span of 30 years. Hard work, but not as hard as working down the pit.

**Norman Ellis**
**July 2002**

**5. East Ardsley Colliery** was sunk c. 1875 by Robert Holliday & Sons. The hotchpotch of structures includes (nearest camera) the screening plant and coal chutes for road wagons. In the vicinity were an iron works and extensive GNR engine sheds. The colliery, seen here c. 1912, was abandoned in 1968.

**6.** Coal was first produced at **Lofthouse Colliery** on the last day of 1877. In the early 1900s, when this photograph was taken, around 1,000 men worked there, many of them from the adjacent village of Outwood. In March 1973, an inrush of water at Kirkhamgate, 3 miles southwest of the pithead, killed seven miners. The colliery closed in 1981.

7. **Liversedge Colliery** was also known as Strawberry Bank Colliery or Dymond's Pit. It lasted from c. 1868 until 1919. This photograph, c. 1911, shows a timber framed headstock, with colliers ready to descend the shaft. The engine house is to the rear.

8. The coking plant at **Liversedge Colliery** was installed in the 1890s. It is shown, c. 1911, with the colliery in the background. Coal was tipped through apertures at the top of the ovens. Coke was scooped out at the side and transferred by barrows to railway trucks.

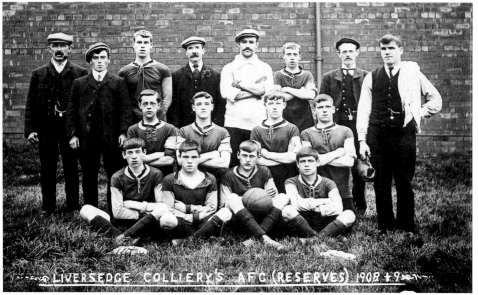

**9. Liversedge Colliery** AFC reserves, 1908/9. Not a smile anywhere. The lads no doubt took the game seriously.

**10.** In the early 1920s, 3,000 people, mostly textile workers and colliers, were out of work in **Batley.** Families were reduced to picking coal from spoil heaps. This street organ was played around the town to raise money for the wives and children of local miners.

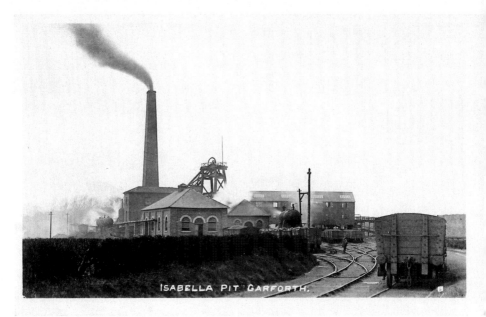

**11.** The Garforth collieries were served by the Aberford Railway. The pits were named after persons. First sunk in 1831-33, **Isabella Pit** took its name from the estate/colliery owner's elder daughter. The pit was worked out by 1925.

**12.** Other Gascoigne-owned pits in the area included Sisters and Elizabeth, named after the owner's younger daughter. The estates eventually passed to the two sisters. Isabella married into the Trench family, hence the name of **Trench Pit** above. Sunk in 1899-1900, it closed in 1925. Both these cards were published by William Bramley of Cross Gates.

**13. Rothwell Haigh** accommodated three collieries, collectively known as J.&J. Charlesworth's Rothwell Haigh Collieries. The one shown, also called Rose Pit, was situated near Rothwell Castle. The image, which includes Carlton Beck, was produced by Bramley of Cross Gates, c. 1925. The colliery closed in 1983.

**14.** Micklefield Coal & Lime company's **Ledston Luck Colliery** began producing in 1912, the likely date of this postcard. Left to right: no. 1 winding house and headgear; compressor house; no. 2 winding house and headgear (upcast). The colliery closed in 1943, the men being moved to the company's Peckfield Colliery. Ledston Luck reopened in 1950, finally closing in 1986.

COMBS COLLIERY, THORNHILL.

**15. Thornhill Combs Colliery** witnessed a severe explosion in 1893, when 139 men and boys were killed. It is pictured here, c. 1920. Closure came in 1972. *"We are going round the pits tomorrow, today we are going round the cloth mills at Dewsbury"*, wrote Amy when she posted the card from Dewsbury to Leighton, Bedfordshire, in August 1929.

SHAW, CROSS. COLLIERY.

**16.** Located just within the Dewsbury boundary amidst fairly rural surroundings, **Shaw Cross Colliery** was sunk in 1903 and abandoned in 1968. This Crawshaw & Warburton pit is seen here from Owl Lane c. 1914.

**17. Old Roundwood Colliery** and the adjacent brickworks each originated in the early 1850s. By 1862, a colliery branch linked the pit with the Great Northern Railway at Low Laithes. The begrimed scene, showing colliery and brickworks (part), appeared on a card posted from Ossett to Arras, France, on 31st December 1908. The site is now an industrial estate.

**18.** Several pits were sunk at Stanley, near Wakefield, where seams of good coal were found. **Newmarket Silkstone Colliery** began producing in c. 1837 and closed in 1983. The opening of the Methley Joint Railway in 1865, which connected with the colliery, enhanced the potential for this and other Charlesworth collieries. The card, by Wallers of Stanley, was issued about 1912.

**19.** This unusual display was the idea of Richard Foster Hilton, a **Skipton** coal merchant. The 'colliery headgear' appears to be topped with a pair of bicycle wheels. The whole contrivance took part in one of the early Skipton Hospital Galas, begun c. 1900.

**20.** Having swept away the dirt and added a few benches, the wagon was deemed ready to take a party on a trip. Rhodes Brothers, coal merchants, operated from Bank Street, **Bradford**. They collected coal from the L&Y (later LMS) coal depot on Spring Mill Street.

**21.** Coal picking at Judy Wood, **Wyke**, near Bradford. The area was said to abound with small mine workings. Here, locals hunt for coal during the 1912 coal strike, which lasted from 1st March to mid-April. The card was posted from Wyke to Morecambe on 4th July 1912.

**22.** Families hunt for coal on a spoil heap near Conyers' Colliery, **Dewsbury Moor,** on 1st April 1912, during the national coal strike. Around Dewsbury, domestic coal became very scarce, whilst mills were either closed or working short time.

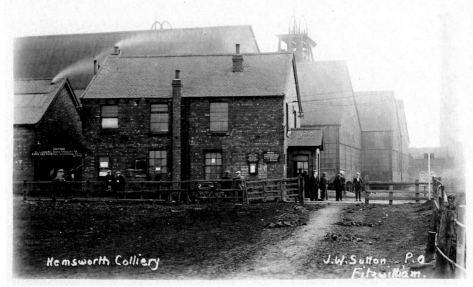

**23.** A notice on the left of this view of **Hemsworth Colliery,** c. 1925, requests that, *"All workmen must search themselves for pipes and matches before entering the cage."* The message on the reverse of the card includes, *"The shaft that can be seen the plainest leads to Haigh Moor Pit. 700 yards deep. Takes just under 1 minute for the cage to go down."*

**24.** A sense of disorder seems to pervade this panorama of **Hemsworth Colliery,** with the coking plant in the foreground. The card was posted from Fitzwilliam, where the colliery was situated, to Brotton, near Saltburn, in 1921. It was worked from 1876 until 1967.

**25.** In 1912, an estimated one million miners went on strike nationwide to secure a guaranteed minimum wage. Coal picking from muck stacks was widespread, as typified here near **Hemsworth Colliery.**

**26.** A soup kitchen was set up behind the Fitzwilliam Hotel in **Hemsworth** during the 1912 strike. The photographer captured these presentable bairns, some wearing Eton collars, displaying their mugs.

**27.** When the owners of Hemsworth Colliery pressed for substantial reductions in rates of pay in 1904-5, colliers withdrew their labour. They and their kin were ordered to vacate colliery-tied houses at **Kinsley**. Many families had to be evicted by the police, as shown here. Some of them found refuge in a hastily devised camp.

**28.** Thomas Elstone, landlord of the Kinsley Hotel, allowed younger children to use the ballroom of the hotel as living quarters during the evictions at **Kinsley**. On 15th September 1905, whilst the ballroom was being cleaned, dinner was served in the courtyard behind the building. An unidentified photographer with initials W.A. captured the pathos.

**29.** This **Hemsworth Colliery** locomotive was photographed during the 1919 coal strike, when sailors were brought in to work the colliery. Joseph Robinson, pit top boss and engineer, is in the cab.

**30.** This locomotive, manufactured by Hudswell Clarke, saw service with the Airedale Colliery Company, which owned three collieries in the **Castleford** area - Allerton Bywater, Fryston and Wheldale.

**31. Whitwood Colliery** of Henry Briggs & Son, viewed from the church tower. Whitwood Lane runs towards Whitwood itself in the distance. The colliery closed in 1968 after a span of 95 years. The card, published by H.M. Wilson of Wood Street, Wakefield, was posted from there to North Finchley in 1913.

**32. Frickley Colliery** at South Elmsall was sunk in 1903. E.L. Scrivens of Doncaster caught this impressive scene in c. 1924. It shows steel lattice headstocks, colliery-owned trucks and wooden pit props. Closure came in 1993, although modernisation had continued almost to the end.

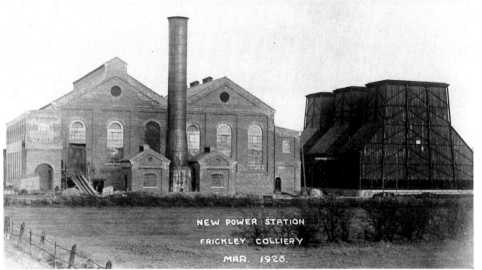

**33.** This power station was constructed adjacent to **Frickley Colliery** in 1925, to supply electric power to that colliery and to other mines of the Carlton Main Colliery Co., including Grimethorpe.

**34.** Part of the interior of the power station at **Frickley,** which includes equipment manufactured by British Thomson-Houston of Rugby. The power station was connected to the National Grid and supplied electricity to some local villages.

**35.** Attempts by the Ferryhill & Rosedale Iron Co. to work **South Kirkby Colliery** failed in 1879. It was reopened in 1881 by the South Kirkby Colliery Co., when the Haigh Moor and Barnsley seams were worked. The colliery closed in 1988. The card, by Barnsley Photo Co., was posted from Pontefract to Henley-on-Thames in 1906.

**36.** Members of the **South Kirkby** branch of the Yorkshire Miners' Association display their banner on a card posted from South Kirkby to Barnsley in 1911. Such banners were proudly blazoned at the various miners' demonstrations.

**37.** On the social side, the village of **South Kirkby** boasted soccer and rugby union teams, several pubs and clubs, a cinema, a miners' institute and the South Kirkby Brass Band, shown here against a local rural background.

**38.** Pastor Belcher was appointed to the Mill Lane Methodist Mission at **South Kirkby** in the 1930s, when a lot of miners were on short time or out of work. Preaching outside pubs, he pursuaded some of the drunken colliers to follow him back to the mission. The postcard, by J. Simonton & Son of Balby, dates from Belcher's time in the village.

**39.** There were collieries in the Altofts area from the early 1850s onwards. This image shows Pope & Pearson's **West Riding Colliery** (also called Diamond Pit) at Altofts, c. 1907. Some idea of the size of the lattice steel headframe and pulleys can be gathered by observing the man on the roof.

**40.** From the late 1860s, Pope & Pearson developed a village settlement at **Altofts** for workers at West Riding Colliery. Its best known feature was Silkstone Row, seen here c. 1904. It comprised 52 three-storey houses with rear yards. The foreground shows part of the miner-initiated Altofts Co-op.

**41.** The Baum washery at Altofts **West Riding Colliery** is visible on the left of this view, with coal hoppers on the right. This and the next photograph were published by G.&J. Hall, Cathedral Studio, Wakefield, in c. 1925.

**42.** The hoppers and chutes for dropping coal into road vehicles at **West Riding Colliery** are featured here in more detail. The last coal was raised from the pit in 1966.

**43.** The Baum mechanised coal-washing plant was installed by Simon-Carves at Altofts **West Riding Colliery** between June 1922 and August 1923. This provided for the washing and grading of coal without it first being manually sorted. The above image and that on the next page, which show the plant under construction, was captured on 26th March 1923.

**44.** A total of 53 postcards were produced to show stages in construction of the washery at **West Riding Colliery.** The cards were discovered in the effects of Albert L. Cox, who was clerk of the colliery, actuary of the colliery bank and a National Union of Mineworkers area secretary. The Yorkshire Penny Bank set up an office at the colliery every Monday evening.

**45. Altofts** Parish Church and the funeral of John Welsby, who had worked at the West Riding Colliery. Welsby was a member of a local rescue team which travelled to Birmingham in the hope of rescuing miners who were trapped following an underground fire at Hamstead Colliery on 4th March 1908.

**46.** When the 26 trapped men at Hamstead Colliery were reached, all of them were dead. John Welsby was overcome by heat and died. Thousands of people attended his funeral in **Altofts** on 14th March 1908. The above facial expressions bring home some of the grief felt.

**47.** In the late afternoon of 27th October 1919, flames were observed coming from the screens surrounding a shaft at **Parkhill Colliery,** Wakefield. Stanley and Wakefield fire brigades were soon in attendance. By late evening, the fire was under control. Wakefield Mines Rescue Station was summoned because of fears for the safety of men working underground.

**48.** The rescuers brought out the trapped colliers via another shaft. There was no loss of life but, as these two photographs show, much damage was caused to surface structures, and many men were thrown out of work. **Parkhill Colliery** lasted until 1982.

**49.** The Nostell Estate, including coal rights, was purchased by the Winn family in 1654. Replacing older workings, **Nostell Colliery** was built in 1865 and is pictured in c. 1905. Visible is an assortment of timber and brick buildings, a wooden headstock, coal wagons and horse-drawn coal carts. Coal production ceased in 1987.

**50.** Clay was frequently found near or amongst coal measures. This, and the availability of coal for baking bricks, were determinant factors in the siting of brickyards near collieries. The brickworks at **Nostell** were opened in 1875 and are shown on a card posted in 1914.

103

LONG ROW, NOSTELL.

**51.** These houses on Long Row, **Nostell,** were built specifically for local colliers by the Winns of Nostell Priory. They were erected in stages from 1860 onwards. The Winns took more than a passing interest in their workers. The card, by W.C. Machan of Wakefield, dates from c. 1912.

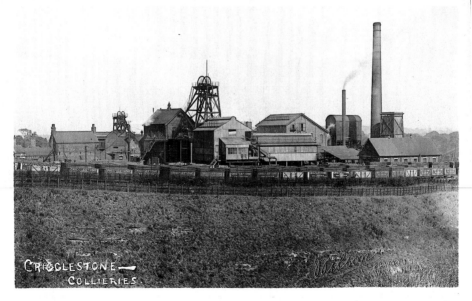

**52.** Originating in the 1890s, **Crigglestone Colliery** and coke-ovens eventually covered a large part of the village. The 1941 explosion, caused by a build-up of the fire-damp during shot-firing, killed 22 men. Housing and an industrial estate now cover the site. The postcard, by H.M. Wilson, Wakefield, is from c. 1912.

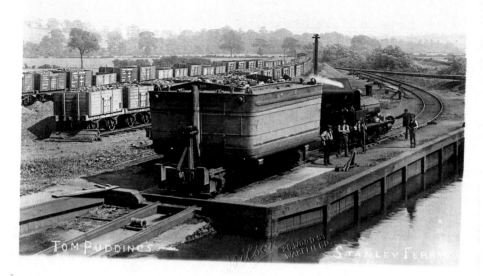

**53.** The Aire & Calder Navigation introduced a unique system for carrying coal in compartment boats known as Tom Puddings. Each unit was conveyed by rail from St. John's Colliery, near Normanton, to **Stanley Ferry** and slipped into the water on its bogie, as is about to happen here.

**54.** Capacity of the compartment boats eventually reached 40 tons each. Up to 19 boats formed a single train. Here, Tom Puddings, pulled by a steam tug with a crew of four, have just left **Stanley Ferry** for Goole. Both these cards were published by H.M. Wilson, photographer, Wakefield, c. 1912.

**55.** Coal-laden Tom Puddings in dock at **Goole** awaiting transfer of their contents into the holds of sea-going ships in c. 1935. Tom Puddings worked from St. John's Colliery until 1942. Postcard by Arjay Productions of Doncaster.

**56. Wakefield** Mines Rescue Station was opened in 1914 on Ings Road. The card by E. Atkinson, photographer, Marygate, Wakefield, shows William Riley (superintendent 1914-50) and his six brigade men. When the station closed in 1986, over 2,000 men had been trained for rescue work throughout the region.

**57.** These Charlesworth coke and by-product works at **Robin Hood** were on the opposite side of the Wakefield-Leeds Road to their colliery. A branch of the East & West Yorkshire Union Railway joined them by means of a level crossing over the road. The colliery and cokeworks survived into nationalisation, but little trace now remains.

**58.** Around 1900, Stringer & Jagger Ltd. opened a coke and by-product plant at Park Gate, on the north side of **Skelmanthorpe** and near their Emley Moor Collieries. The plant is pictured shortly after opening.

*J.A.Stephenson.*

SOUTH QUEEN ST., MORLEY.

**59.** Horse-drawn coal delivery carts such as this were a familiar sight up to the 1940s. Smith obtained his supplies from the Great Northern Railway coal depot in **Morley**. The coal was tipped at factories, mills or houses.

HENRY HANSON. PADDOCK

**60.** The introduction of bagged coal meant that the fuel could be unloaded through cellar grates or into coal sheds. Henry Hanson, above, was a coal merchant and furniture remover in the Paddock area of **Huddersfield**, procuring his supplies from Gledholt sidings.

UPTON COLLY. GENERAL VIEW.

**61.** Construction work at **Upton Colliery** began in 1924. The picture shows no. 1 and no. 2 (nearest camera) shafts and headgear nearing completion. After a chequered life, the National Coal Board filled in the shafts in 1964. Coloured Yorkshire comedian Charlie Williams once worked at this pit.

COPYRIGHT
UTN. 4.

THE UPTON ARMS. UPTON.

LILYWHITE LTD.
TRIANGLE. HALIFAX

**62.** The coming of the colliery changed the face of **Upton.** A programme of housebuilding was begun by the Upton Coal Co. Clubs and pubs were erected. "The Upton Arms," shown here, was opened in 1927. The Lilywhite card, posted from Upton in 1942, includes the message, *"Going to the dance at the Upton Arms tonight."*